# all woman

## VOLUME TWO

Lillo's Music
10848 - 82 Ave.
Edmonton, AB
T6E 2B3 (403-433-0138)

**IMP**

**International MUSIC Publications**

International Music Publications Limited
Griffin House 161 Hammersmith Road London W6 8BS England

D0619667

DON'T BE
A MUSIC
COPYCAT!

The copying of © copyright
material is a criminal offence
and may lead to prosecution.

Series Editor: Sadie Cook

Editorial, production and recording: Artemis Music Limited
Design and Production: Space DPS Limited

Published 2000

International
MUSIC
Publications

© International Music Publications Limited
Griffin House 161 Hammersmith Road London W6 8BS England

Reproducing this music in any form is illegal and forbidden by
the Copyright, Designs and Patents Act 1988

International Music Publications Limited

**England:**     Griffin House
                 161 Hammersmith Road
                 London W6 8BS

**Germany:**     Marstallstr. 8
                 D-80539 München

**Denmark:**     Danmusik
                 Vognmagergade 7
                 DK1120 Copenhagen K

Carisch

**Italy:**       Via Campania 12
                 20098 San Giuliano Milanese
                 Milano

**Spain:**       Magallanes 25
                 28015 Madrid

**France:**      20 Rue de la Ville-l'Eveque
                 75008 Paris

# all woman

## VOLUME TWO

# Anytime You Need A Friend

Words and Music by
Mariah Carey and Walter Afanasieff

© 1993 & 2000 Wallyworld Music, WB Music Corp, Rye Songs and Sony Songs Inc, USA
Warner/Chappell Music Ltd, London W6 8BS and Sony/ATV Music Publishing, London W1V 2LP

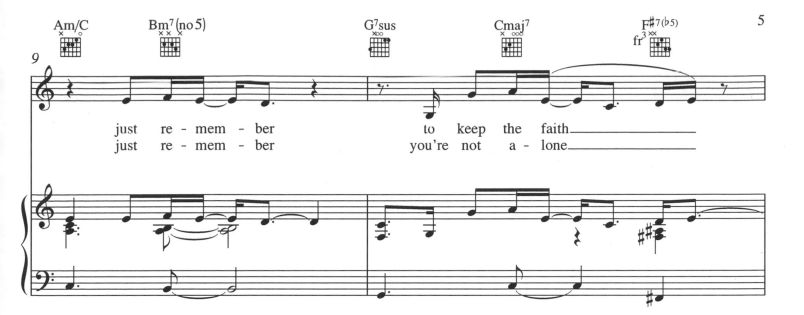

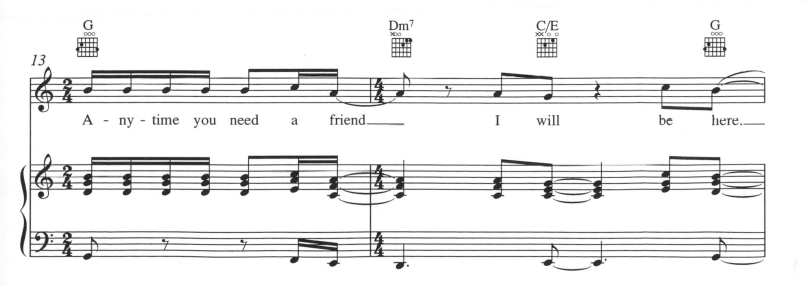

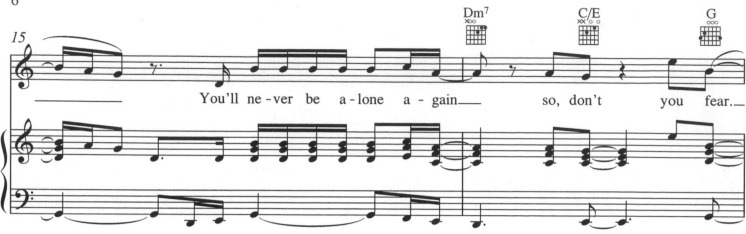

You'll ne-ver be a-lone a-gain___ so, don't you fear.___

E-ven if you're miles a-way,___ I'm by your side.___

So, don't you ev-er be lone-ly.

Love will make it al-right.___

I will be here._____ You'll ne-ver be a-lone a-gain__

so, don't you fear._____ E-ven if you're miles a-way,__

I'm by your side._____ So, don't you ev - er be

*Repeat and fade*

lone - ly. It's al-right. It's al-right. A - ny-time you need a friend__

# Don't It Make
# My Brown Eyes Blue

Words and Music by
Richard Leigh

© 1977 & 2000 EMI Catalogue Partnership and EMI U Catalog Inc, USA
Worldwide print rights controlled by Warner Bros Publications Inc/IMP Ltd

give me no rea - sons, give me a - li - bies. Tell me you love me and don't_

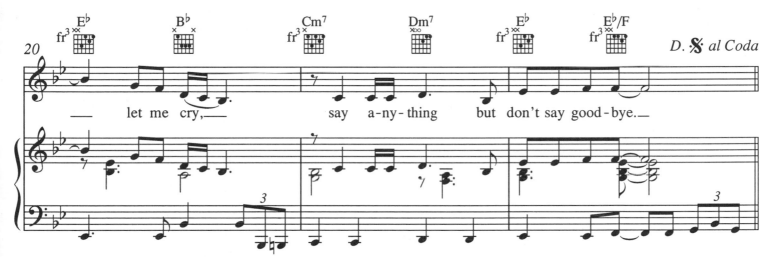

_ let me cry,___ say a-ny-thing but don't say good-bye._

D. %. al Coda

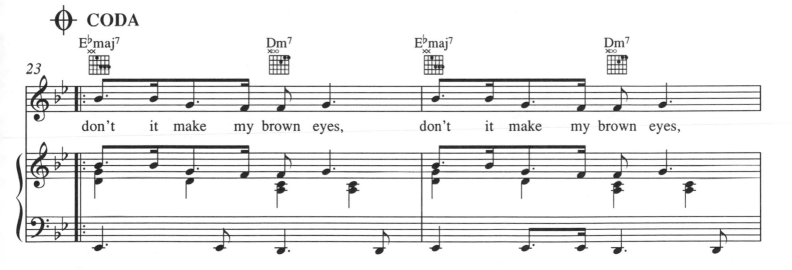

**CODA**

don't it make my brown eyes, don't it make my brown eyes,

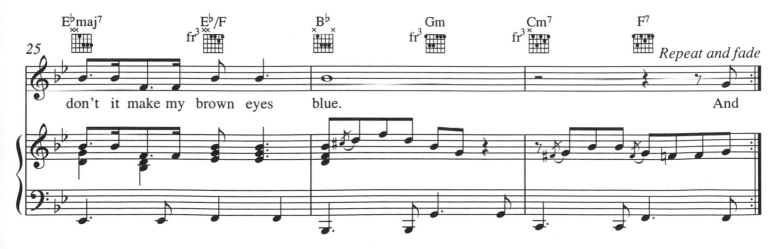

*Repeat and fade*

don't it make my brown eyes blue. And

# Flashdance . . . What A Feeling

Words by Keith Forsey
Music by Irene Cara and Giorgio Moroder

**Steadily**

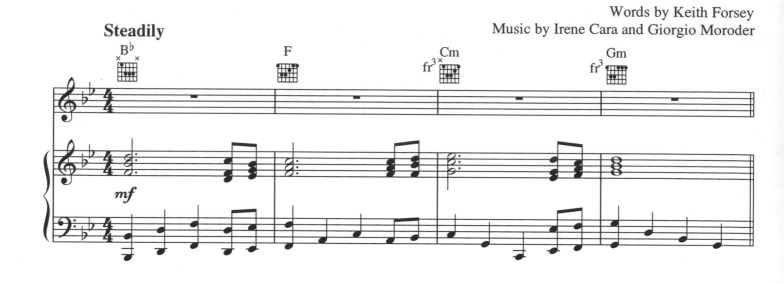

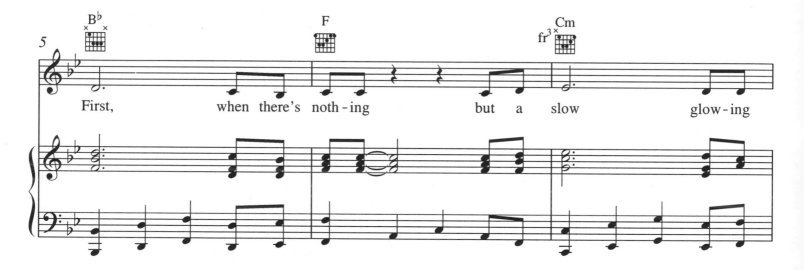

First, when there's noth-ing but a slow glow-ing

dream,____ that your fear seems to hide deep in -

© 1983 & 2000 Intersong USA Inc, Famous Music Corp and Giorgio Moroder Publishing Co, USA
Warner/Chappell Music Ltd, London W6 8BS

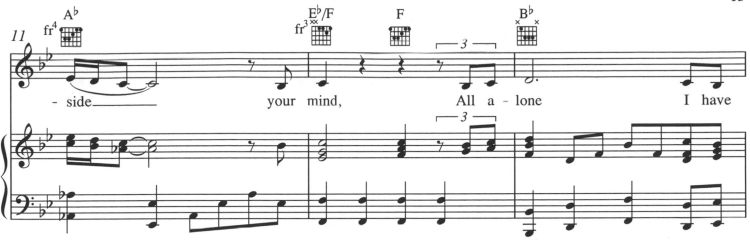

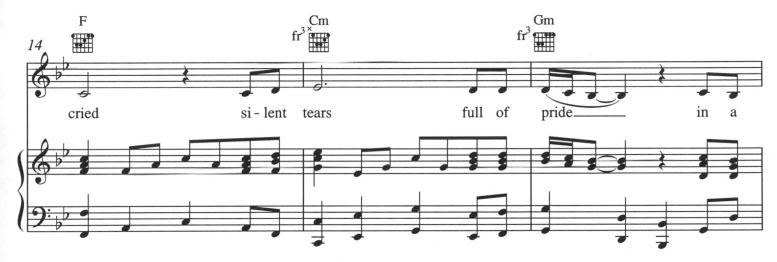

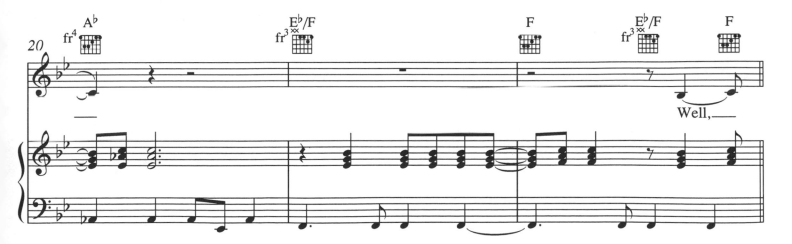

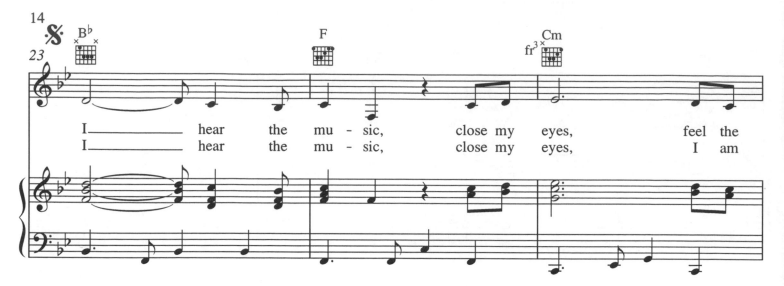

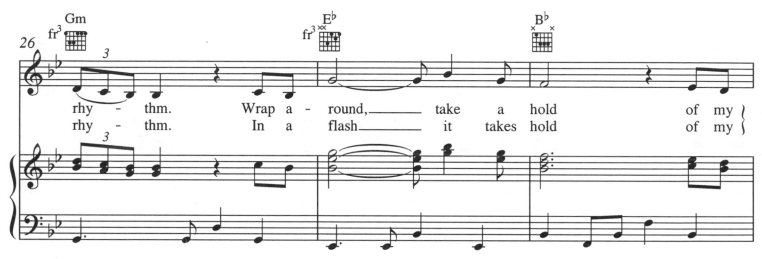

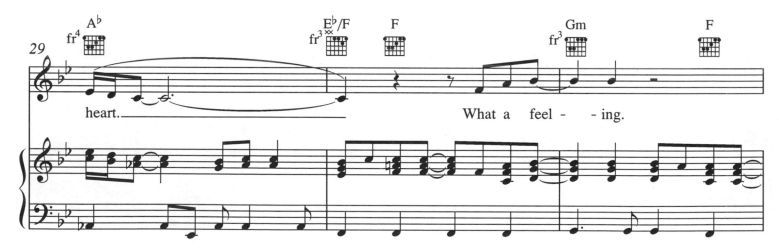

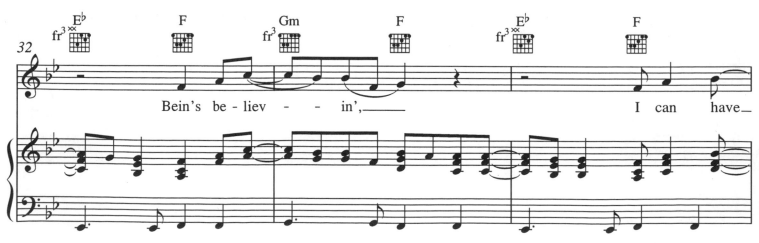

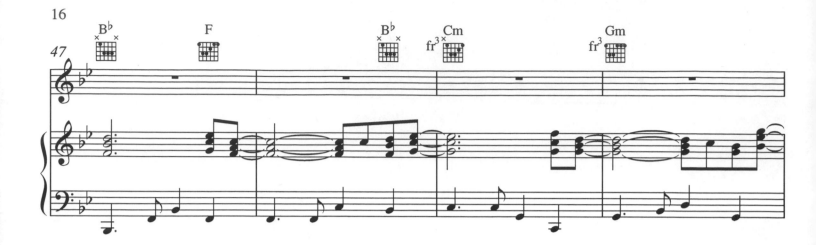

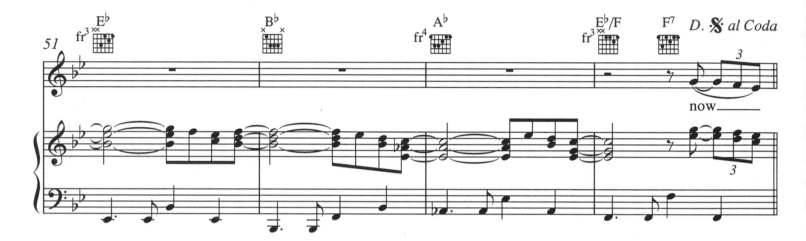

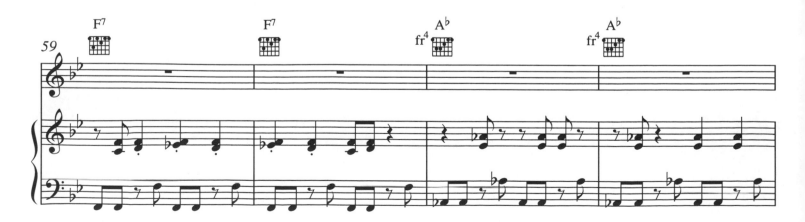

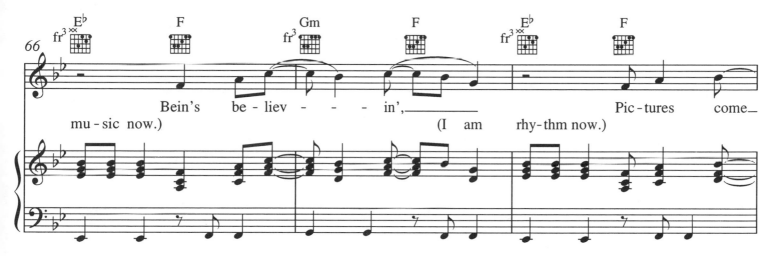

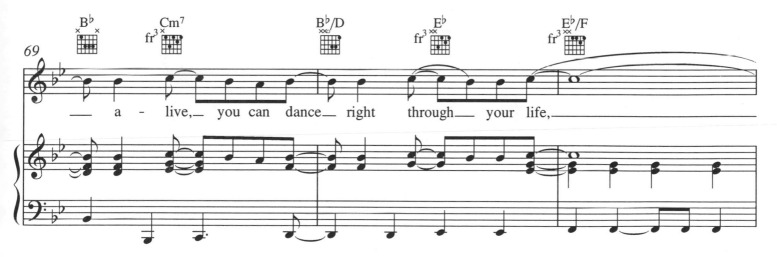

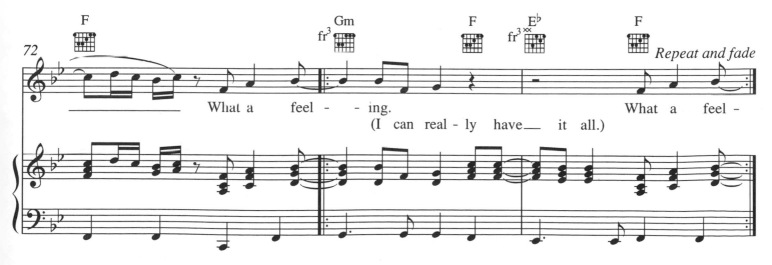

# I'll Stand By You

Words and Music by Billy Steinberg,
Tom Kelly and Chrissie Hynde

© 1994 & 2000 Jerk Awake, Tom Kelly Songs and Clive Banks Songs
EMI Music Publishing Ltd and EMI Music Publishing Ltd trading as Clive Banks Songs, London WC2H 0EA

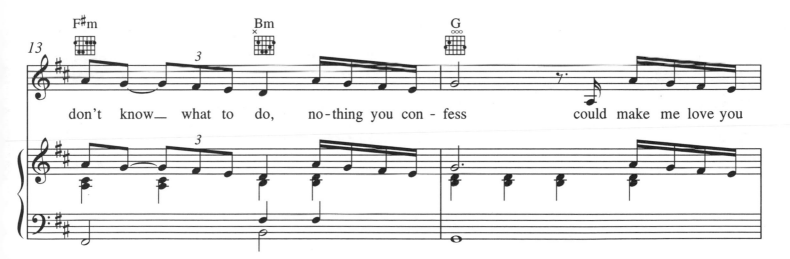

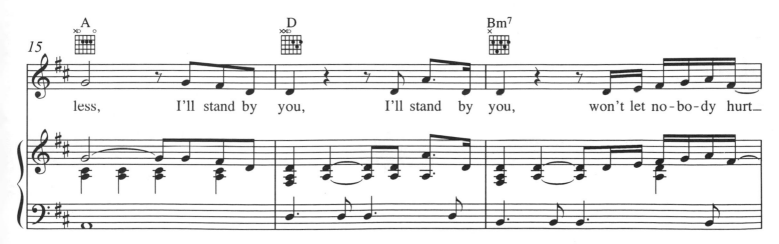

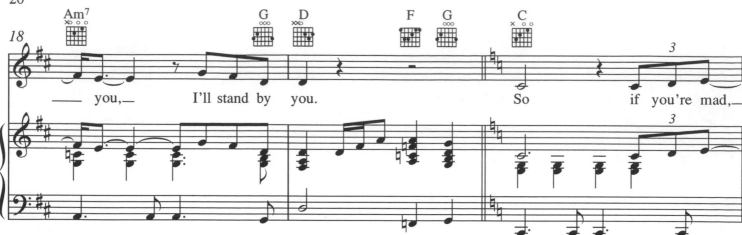

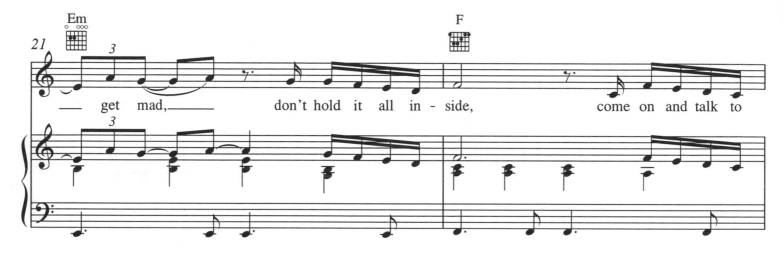

you,___ I'll stand by you. So if you're mad,___

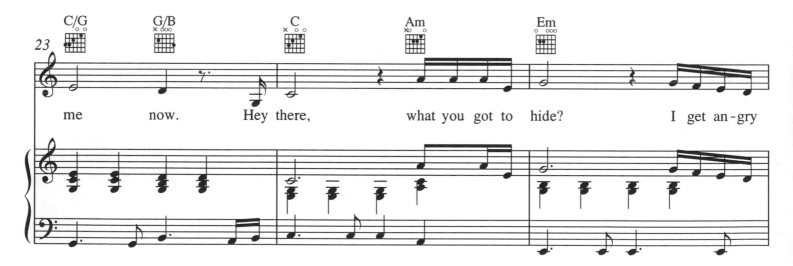

___ get mad,_____ don't hold it all in - side, come on and talk to

me now. Hey there, what you got to hide? I get an - gry

too, well, I'm a - lone like you.___ When you're

stand - ing____ at the cross - roads, and don't know which path to choose, let me come a -

-long, 'cause e - ven if you're wrong I'll stand by

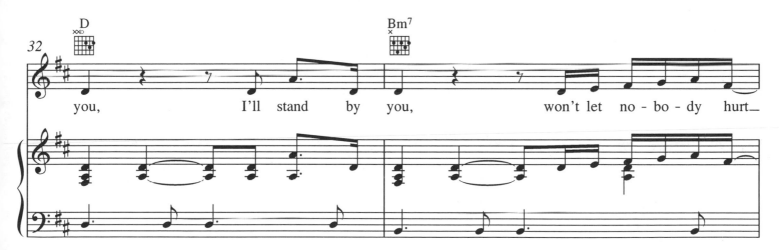

you, I'll stand by you, won't let no - bo - dy hurt____

____ you,____ I'll stand by you, ba - by, e - ven to your

22

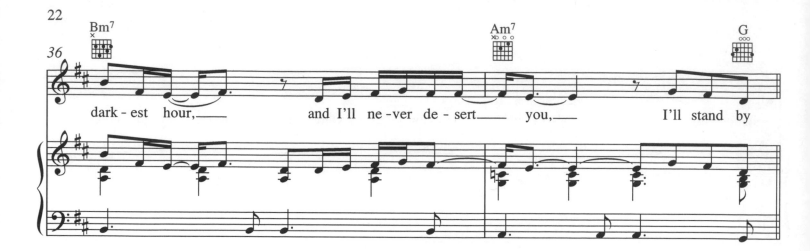

dark - est hour,_____ and I'll ne -ver de - sert_____ you,_____ I'll stand by

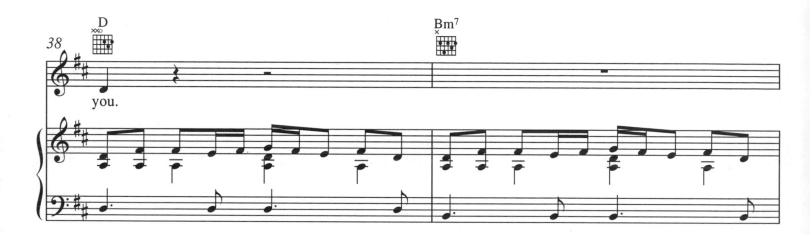

you.

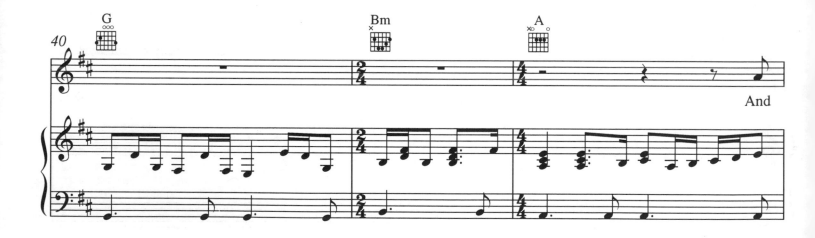

And

when, when the night falls_____ on you ba - by, you're feel-ing all a -

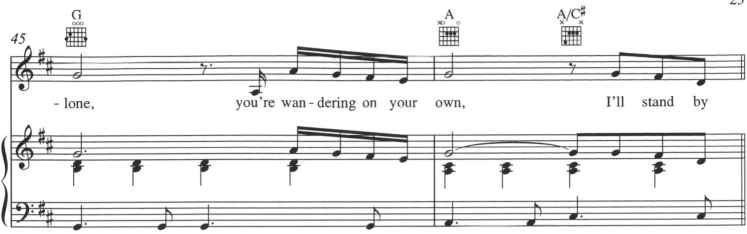

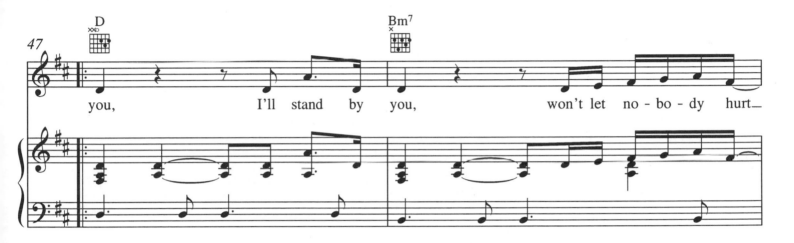

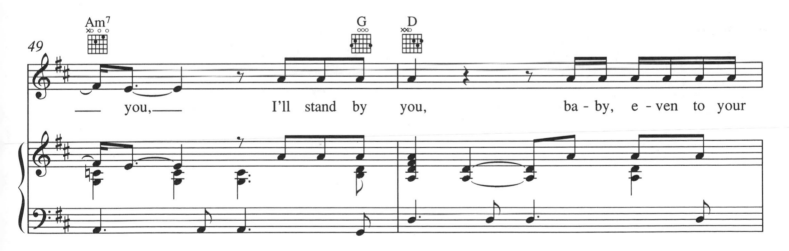

# Killing Me Softly With His Song

Tempo rubato

Words by Norman Gimbel
Music by Charles Fox

© 1972 & 1999 Fox-Gimbel Productions Inc, USA
Onward Music Ltd, London W8 7TQ

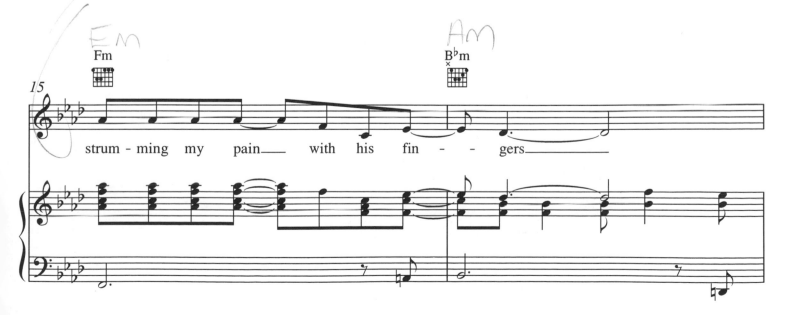

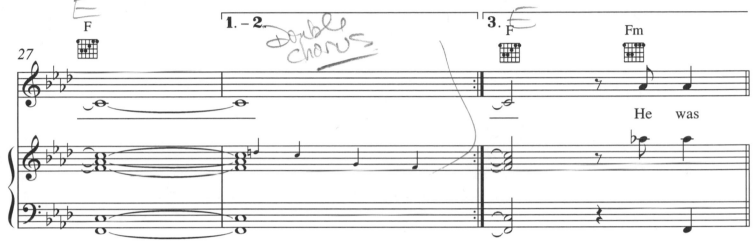

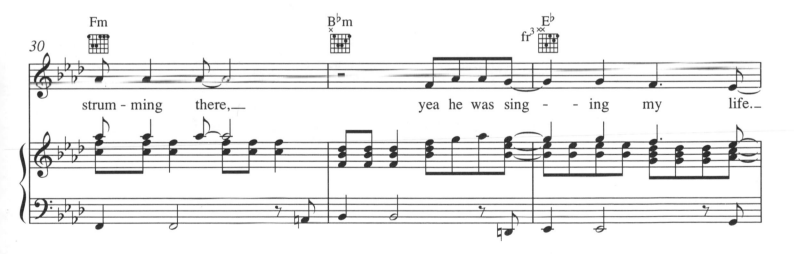

# One Moment In Time

Words and Music by
John Hammond and Albert Hammond

© 1988 & 2000 John Bettis Music, Albert Hammond Enterprises and WB Music Corp, USA
Warner/Chappell Music Ltd, London W6 8BS and Windswept Pacific Music Ltd, London W11 4SQ

time, when I'm rac - ing__ with des - ti - ny, then in that__ one

mo - ment__ in __ time, I will feel, I will feel e - ter - ni -

-ty. (3.) I've lived to feel e - ter - ni -

-ty. You're a win - ner for a life - time,

if you seize that_ one mo - ment in time, make_ it

a tempo

rall.

shine. Give me__ one mo - ment_ in time when I'm

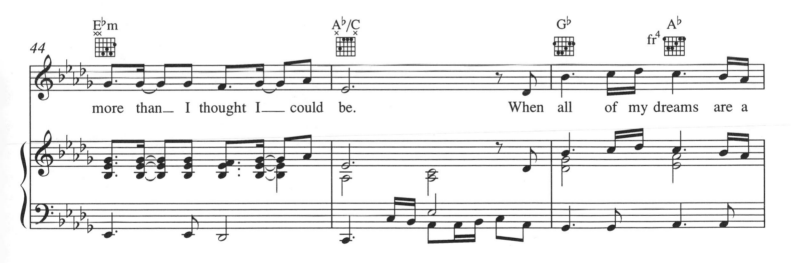

more than_ I thought I__ could be. When all of my dreams are a

heart - beat a - way and the an - swers are all up_ to me._ Give_ me__

one   mo - ment__ in time          when I'm   rac - ing__  with  des - ti -

-ny.__          Then      in that_ one   mo - ment__ in__ time,       I will

be,      I____ will      be,__      I will be   free.__

I   will   be, I will  be   free.__

# Pearl's A Singer

Words and Music by Ralph Dino,
Mike Sembello, Jerry Leiber and Mike Stoller

© 1974, 1977 (renewed) & 2000 Jerry Leiber Music and Mike Stoller Music, USA
Carlin Music Corp, London NW1 8BD

sing-er,___ she sings songs___ for the lost___ and the lone-
sing-er,___ and they say___ that she once___ cut a re-

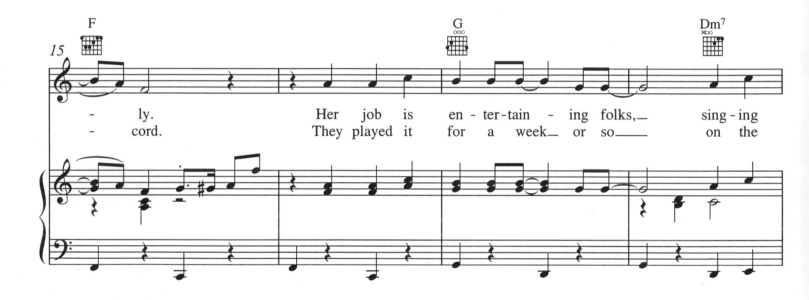

F                             G                   Dm7

- ly.          Her job is en-ter-tain - ing folks,___ sing-ing
- cord.       They played it for a week___ or so___ on the

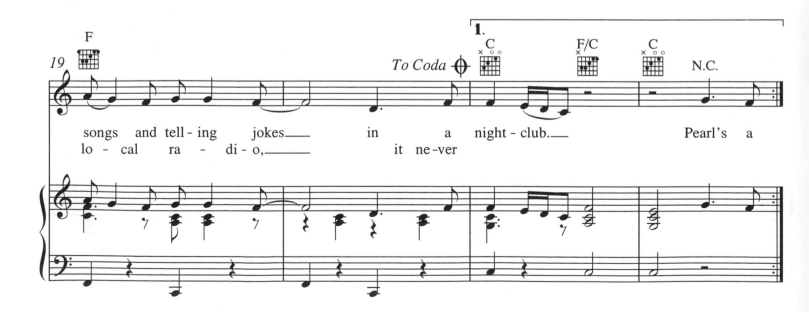

F                                  **1.**
                                  C         F/C      C
*To Coda* ⊕                              N.C.

songs and tell-ing jokes___ in a night - club.___ Pearl's a
lo - cal ra - di - o,___ it ne-ver

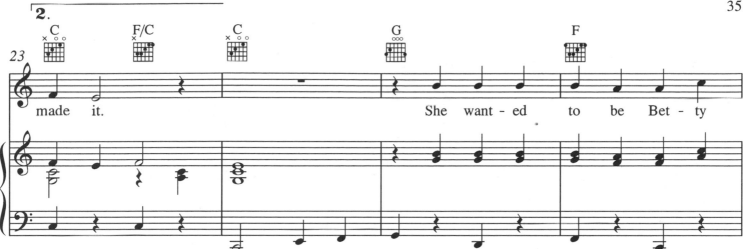

made it. She want-ed to be Bet-ty

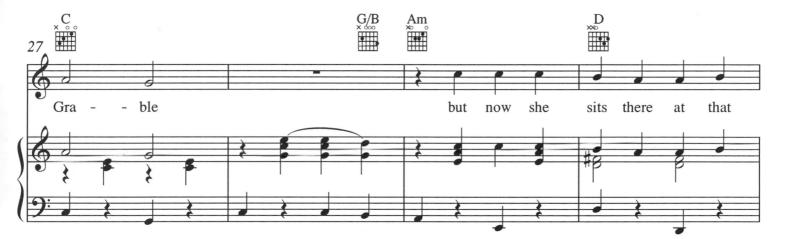

Gra——ble but now she sits there at that

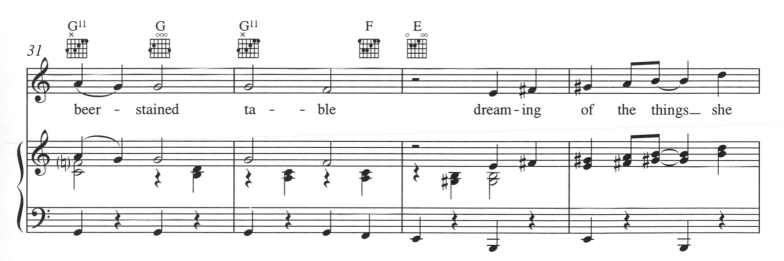

beer-stained ta——ble dream-ing of the things— she

ne-ver got to do,___ all those dreams___ that ne-ver___ came

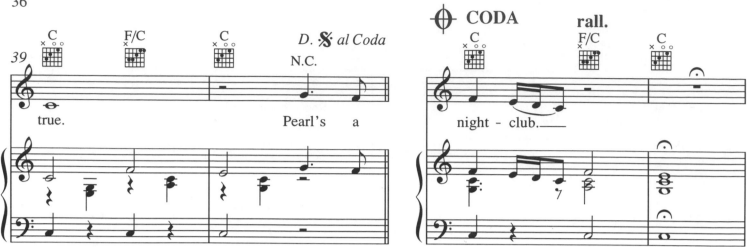

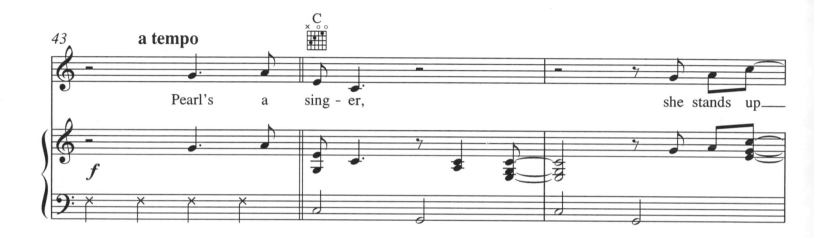

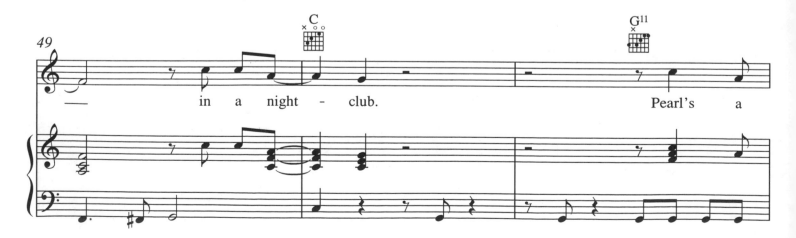

sing - er, she sings songs___ for the lost___

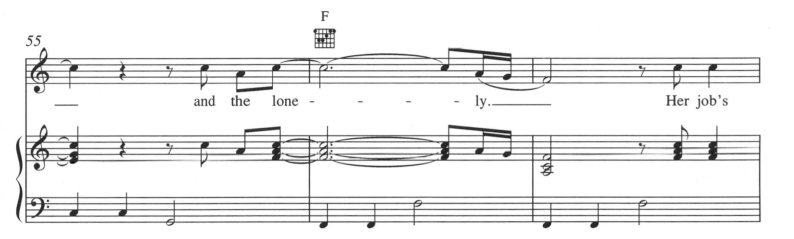

___ and the lone - - - - ly.___ Her job's

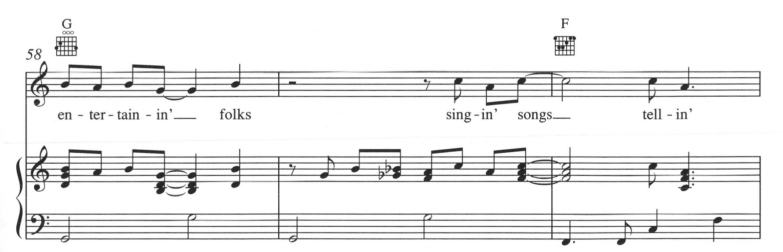

en - ter - tain - in'___ folks sing - in' songs___ tell - in'

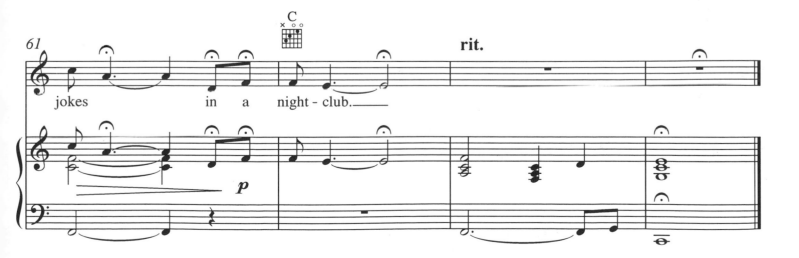

jokes in a night - club.___

**rit.**

*p*

# (They Long To Be) Close To You

Words by Hal David
Music by Burt Bacharach

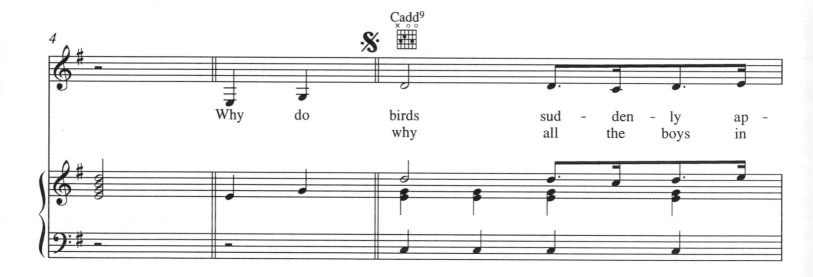

© 1963 & 2000 New Hidden Valley Music and Casa David Music, USA
Warner/Chappell Music Ltd, London W6 8BS

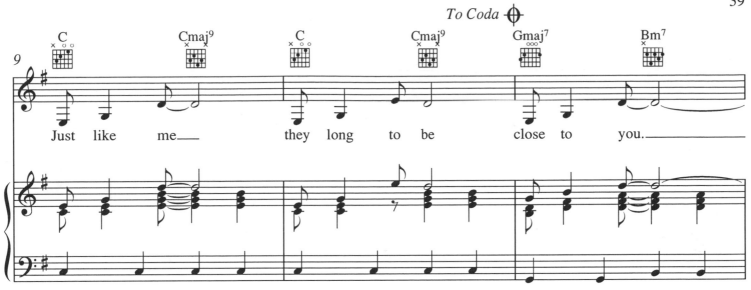

Just like me___ they long to be close to you.___

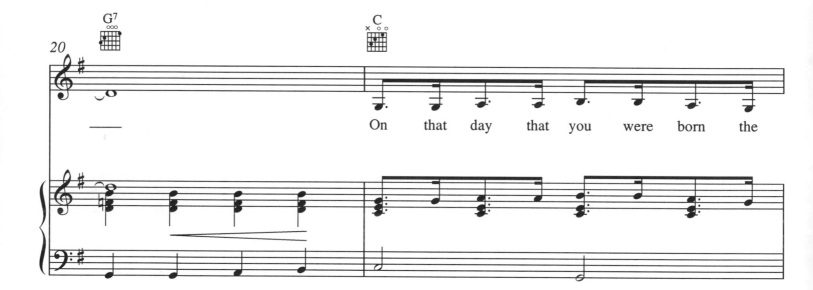

___ On that day that you were born the

an - gels got to - ge - ther,___ And de - cid - ed to cre - ate a dream come

# Think

Words and Music by
Ted White and Aretha Franklin

© 1968 & 2000 Fourteenth Hour Music Corp and Pundit Music, USA
EMI Songs Ltd, London WC2H 0EA

let your-self be free.— Let's go back— let's go back, let's go

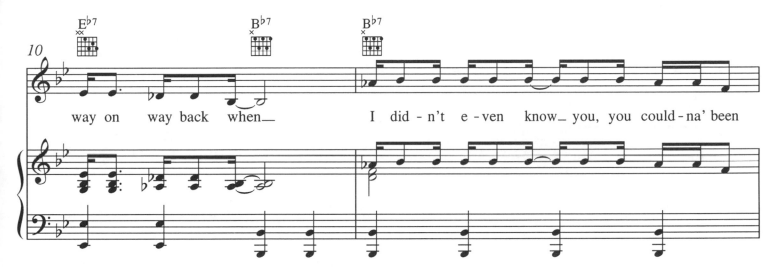

way on way back when— I did-n't e-ven know— you, you could-na' been

too much more than ten.— I ain't no— psy-chi-a-trist, I ain't no

doc-tor with de-grees— but it don't take— too much high I. Q.—

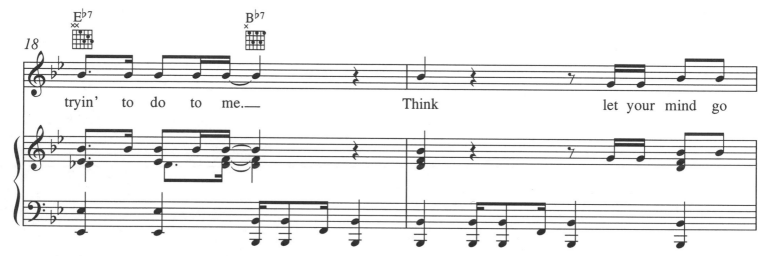

free - dom___ (free-dom) oh,___ free - dom___ (free-dom). Gim-me some

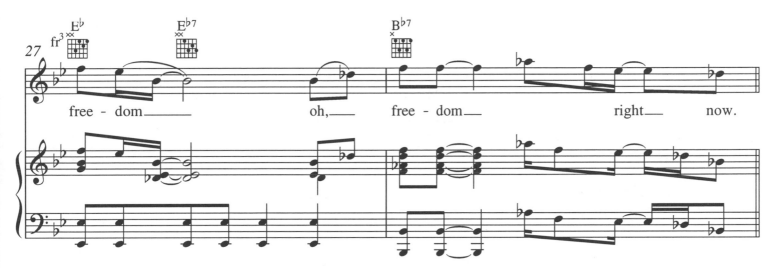

free - dom_____ oh,___ free-dom___ right___ now.

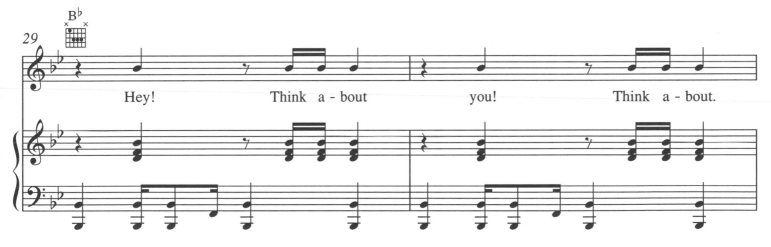

Hey! Think a-bout you! Think a-bout.

There ain't no-thin' you could ask___ I could an-swer you___ with I want_____ but

**41**

to make o-ther peo-ple lose their minds, well, be care-ful you don't lose yours, oh

*D. %: al Coda*

**CODA**

**43**

You need me___ and I need you___ with-

**45**

-out each o-----ther, there ain't noth-in' ei----ther can do. Oh,___

**47**

*Repeat and fade*

hey think a-bout me. (To the bone for deepness.)

# True Blue

Words and Music by
Madonna Ciccone and Stephen Bray

© 1986 & 2000 WB Music Corp, Bleu Disque Music Co Inc, Webo Girl Publishing Inc and Black Lion Music Inc, USA
Warner/Chappell Music Ltd, London W6 8BS and Universal/Island Music Ltd, London W6 8JA

- -ver knew love___ be - fore ___ 'til you walked
___ they won't fall___ a - gain. I'm so ex - cit - ed 'cause

through my door. I've___
you're my best friend. So___

___ had o - - ther lips; I've___
if you should ev - er doubt; won - der what___

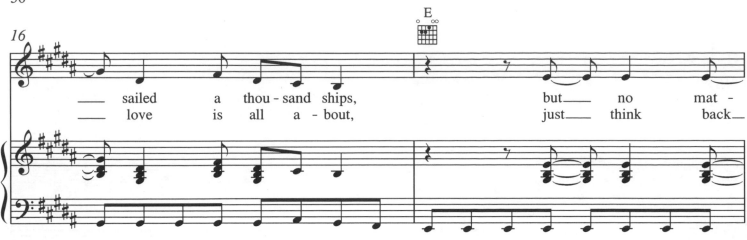

like a glove._____ And I'm gon-na be true blue, ba-by.

I love you.__ true blue, ba-by. I love you.__'Cause it's

true love;_____ you're the one I'm__ dream-ing of._____

*Counter-melody*

This time I know it's true love; you're the one I'm

Your heart fits me like a glove._____ And I'm gon-na be

dream - ing of._____ Heart fits me like a glove._____

true blue, ba-by. I love you.__ No, no more

sad - ness I kiss it good - bye. The sun__ is burst -

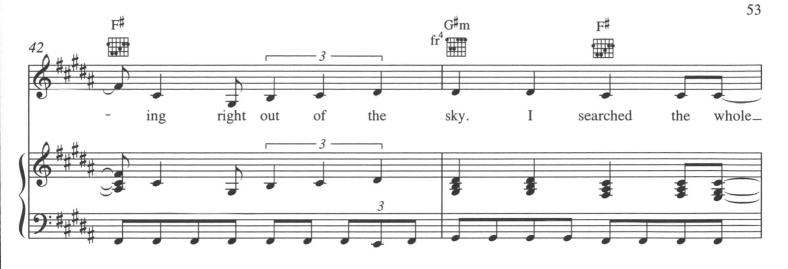

-ing right out of the sky. I searched the whole—

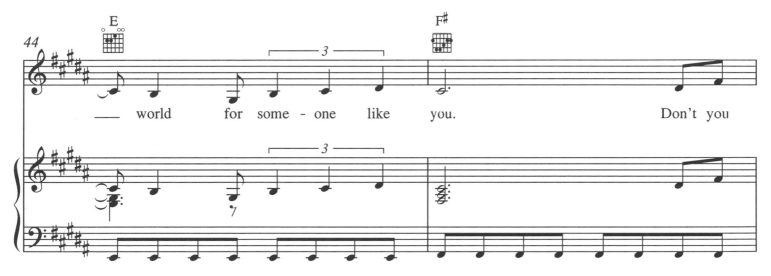

— world for some - one like you. Don't you

know, don't you know that's it's true, love.— Oh ba - by,

true love,— oh ba-by. Oh love,— oh ba-by, true love. It's

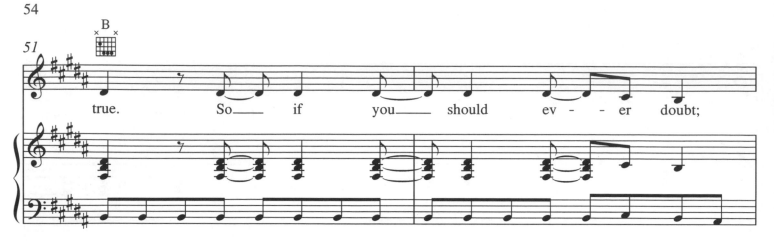

true. So__ if you__ should ev - - er doubt;

won - der what__ love is all a-bout. Just think back and__

__ re - mem - ber, dear, those words whis-pered in your ear.__ I said,

True love;_____ you're the one I'm__ dream-ing of._____

*Counter-melody*

This love I know it's true love; you're the one I'm

# Walk On By

Words by Hal David
Music by Burt Bacharach

© 1964 & 1999 New Hidden Valley Music and Casa David Music, USA
Warner/Chappell Music Ltd, London W6 8BS

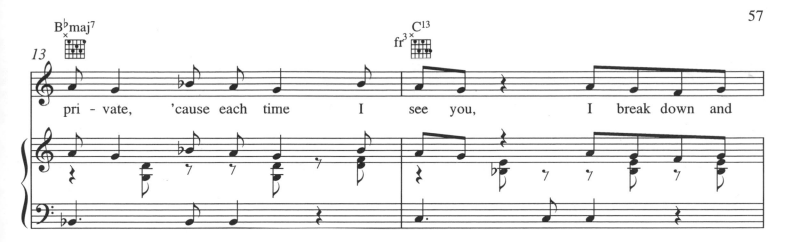

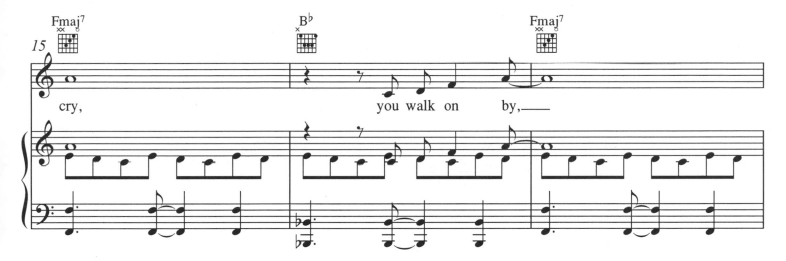

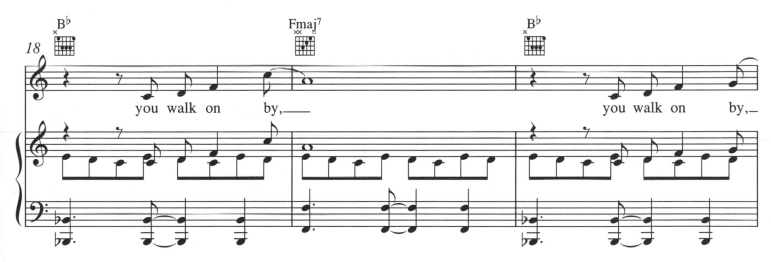

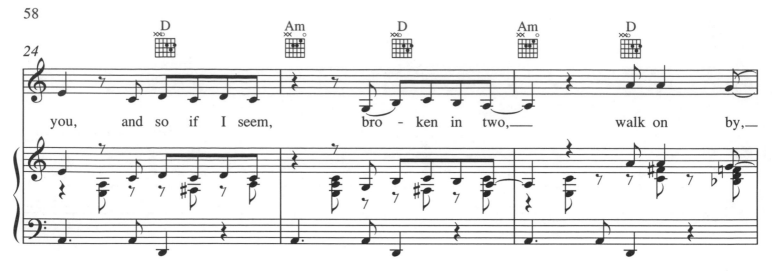

you, and so if I seem, bro - ken in two,___ walk on by,___

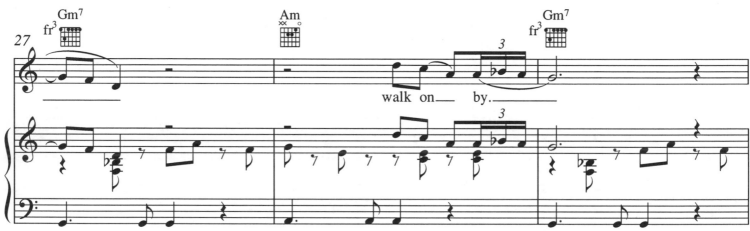

walk on___ by.___

Fool - ish pride,___ that's all that I have left, so let me hide___ the

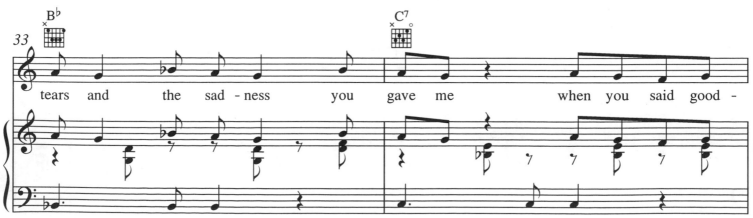

tears and the sad - ness you gave me when you said good -

-bye, aye, aye, aye. So walk on by,

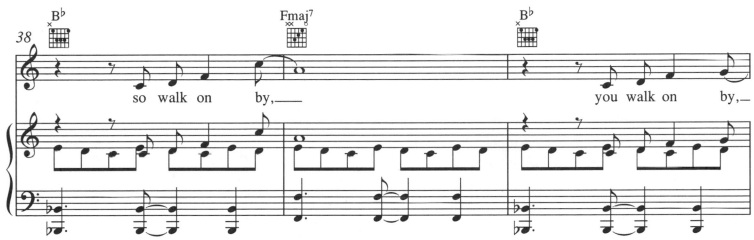

so walk on by, you walk on by,

so walk on by,

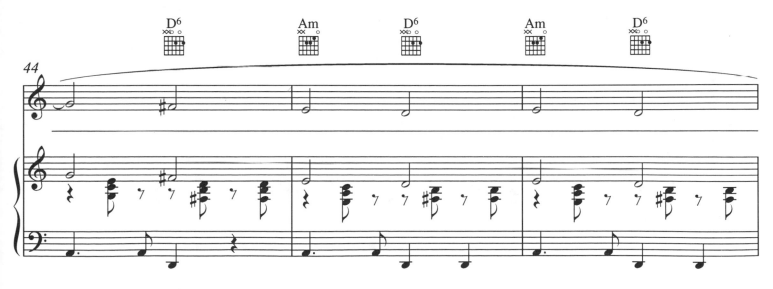

60

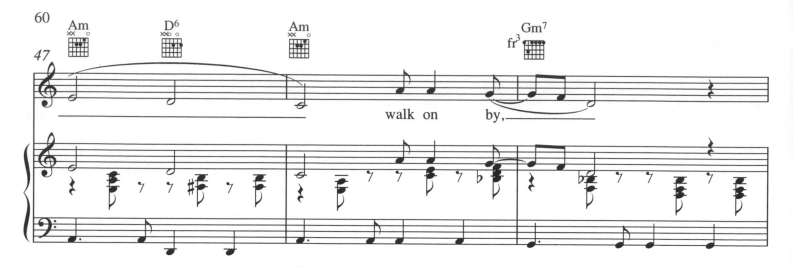

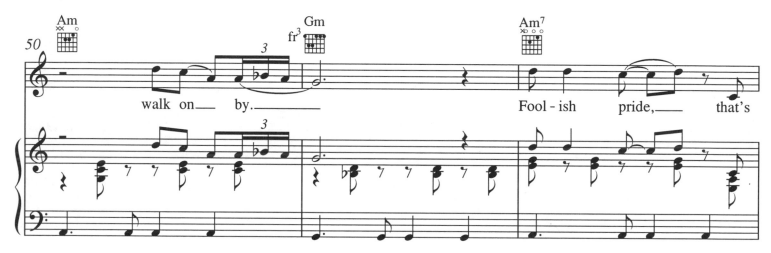

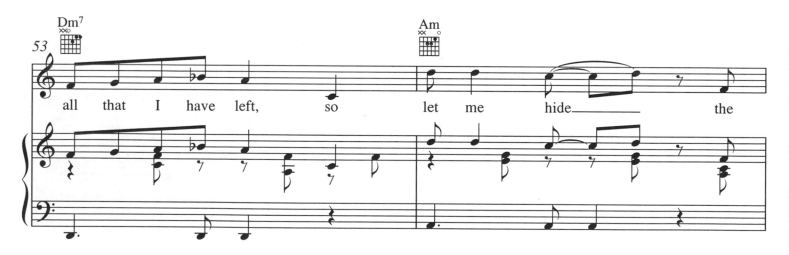

- bye, aye, aye, aye.＿＿＿ So walk on by,＿

＿ so walk on by,＿

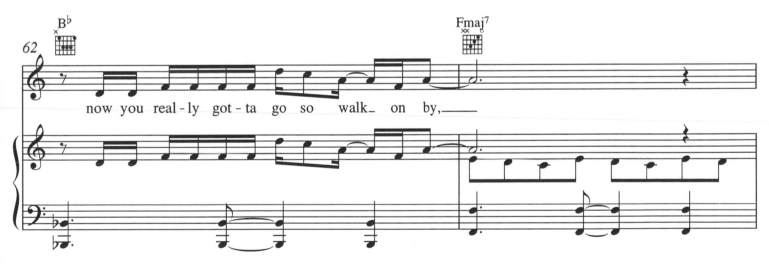

now you real-ly got-ta go so walk on by,＿

take your leave, you'll ne-ver see those tears that cry.＿

# The Wind Beneath My Wings

Words and Music by
Larry Henley and Jeff Silbar

© 1981, 1983 & 1999 Warner House of Music and WB Gold Music Corp, USA
Warner/Chappell Music Ltd, London W6 8BS

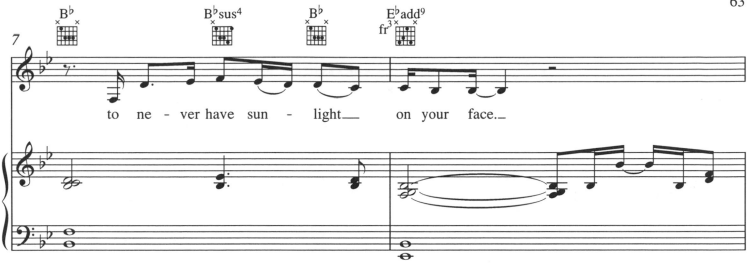

to ne - ver have sun - light___ on your face.__

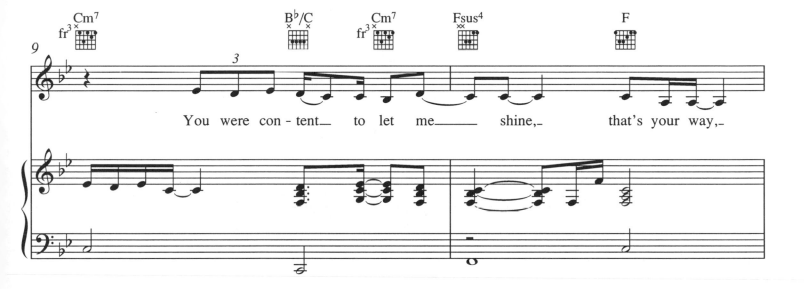

You were con - tent___ to let me___ shine,_ that's your way,_

you al - ways walked a step_ be - - hind.__

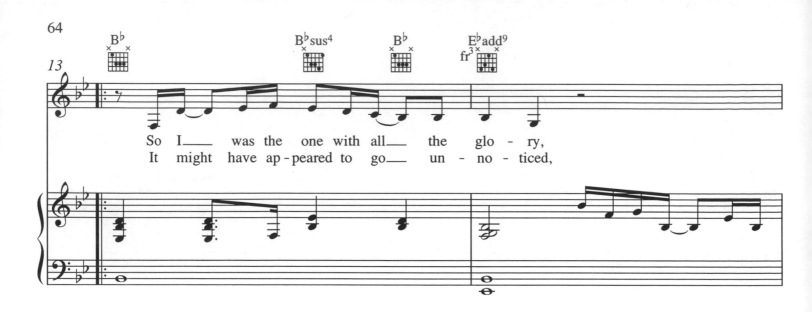

So I___ was the one with all___ the glo - ry,
It might have ap - peared to go___ un - no - ticed,

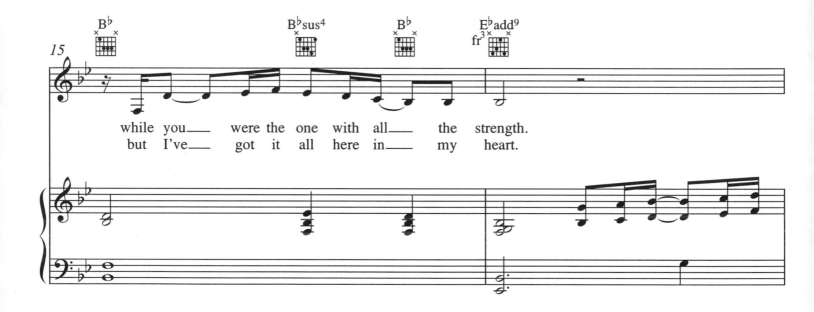

while you___ were the one with all___ the strength.
but I've___ got it all here in___ my heart.

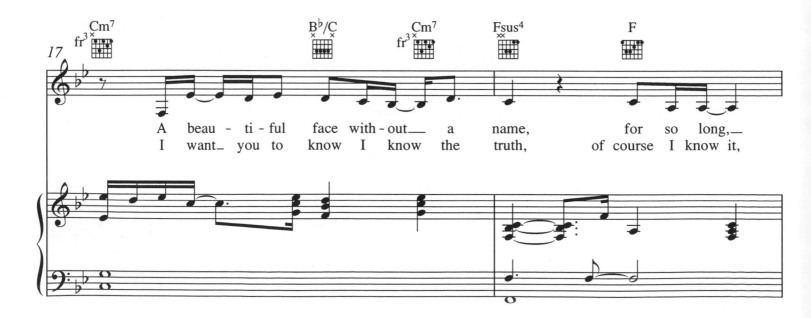

A beau - ti - ful face with - out___ a name,     for so long,___
I want___ you to know I know the truth,     of course I know it,

'cause you are the wind be - neath my wings.

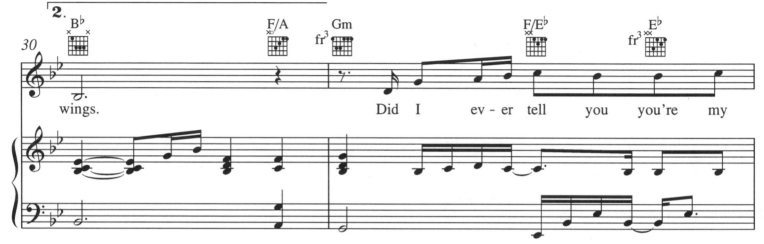

wings. Did I ev - er tell you you're my

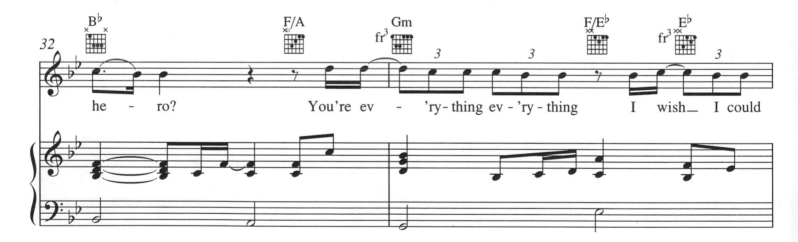

he - ro? You're ev - 'ry - thing ev - 'ry - thing I wish I could

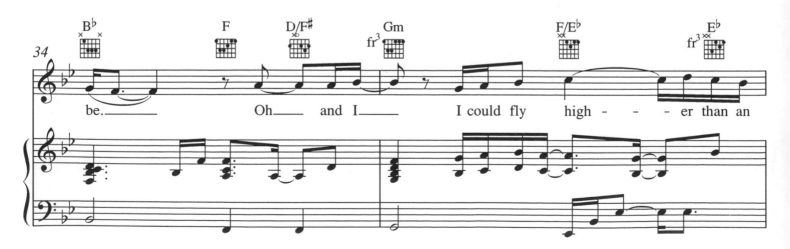

be. Oh and I I could fly high - - er than an

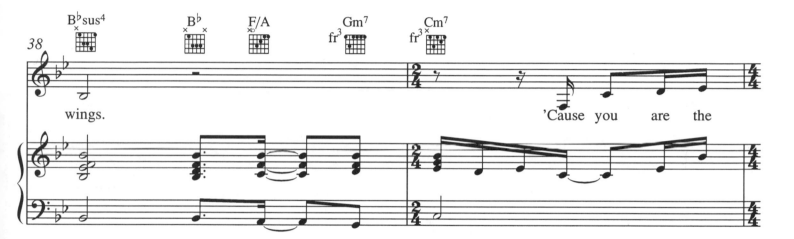

68

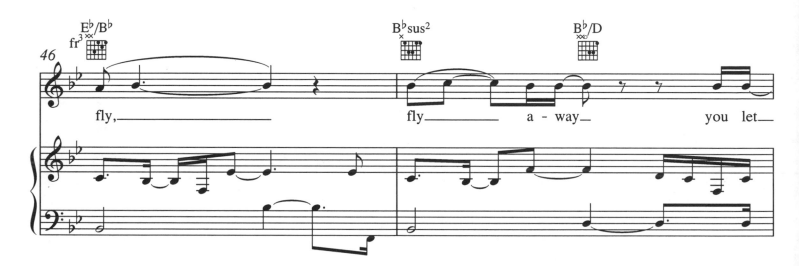

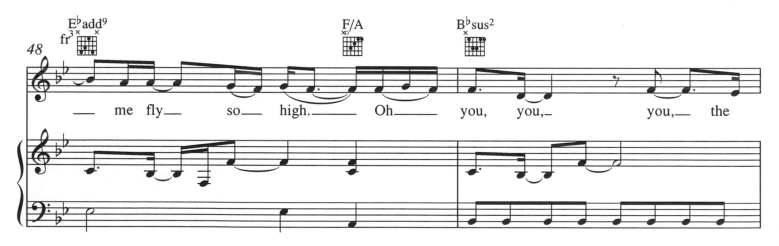

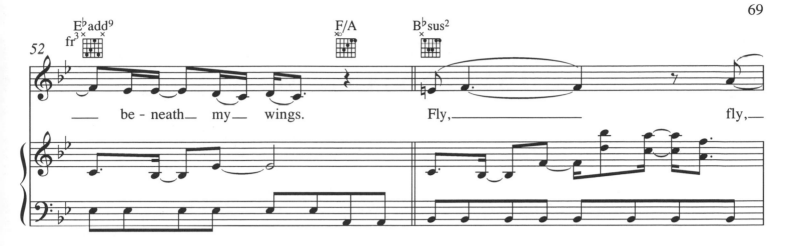

be - neath my wings. Fly,_____ fly,____

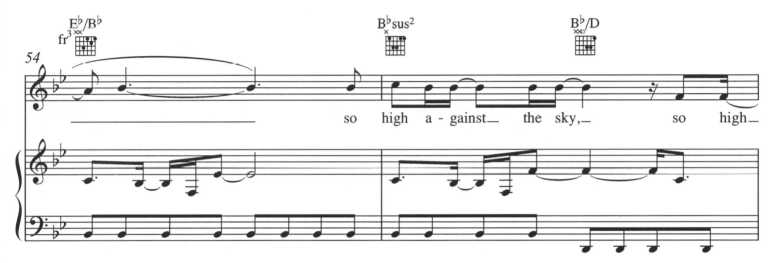

_____ so high a - gainst the sky,___ so high___

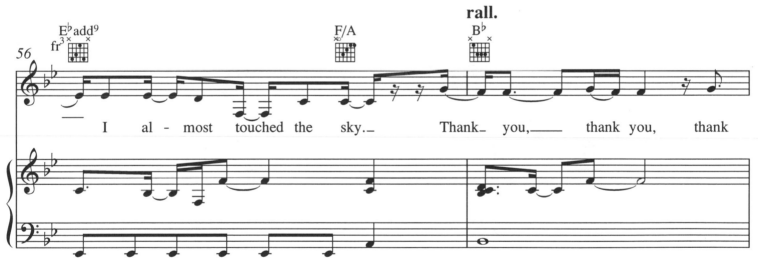

__ I al - most touched the sky.__ Thank_ you,___ thank you, thank

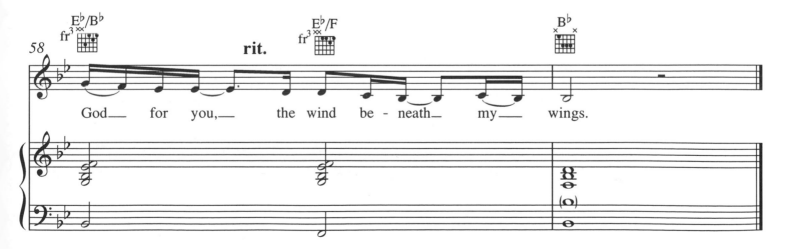

God__ for you,___ the wind be - neath__ my___ wings.

# You Don't Have To Say You Love Me

Original Words by Vito Pallavicini
English Words by Vicki Wickham and Simon Napier-Bell
Music by Pino Donaggio

© 1965 & 2000 Edizioni Musicali Accordo SRL, Italy
Worldwide print rights controlled by Warner Bros Publications Inc/IMP Ltd and B Feldman & Co Ltd, London WC2H 0EA

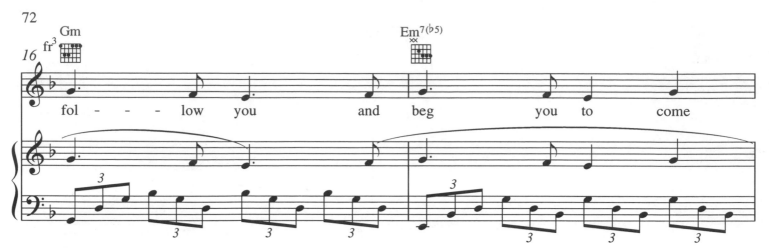

fol - - - low you and beg you to come

home. You don't have to say you love me

just be close at hand, you don't have to stay for - ev - er

I will un - der - stand,___ be - lieve me,___ be - lieve me___ I

can't help but love you___ but be - lieve me I'll ne - ver___ tie you

down._____ Left a - lone with just a

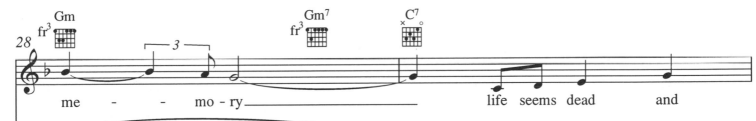

me - - mo - ry_____ life seems dead and

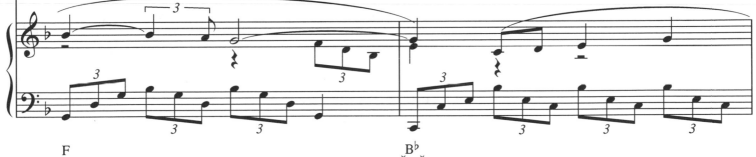

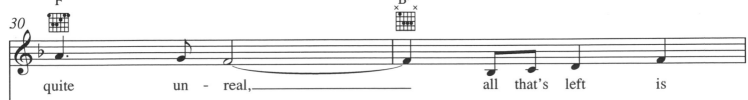

quite un - real,_____ all that's left is

# 1-2-3

Words and Music by
Gloria Estefan and Enrique E Garcia

**Bright dance tempo** ♩ = 120

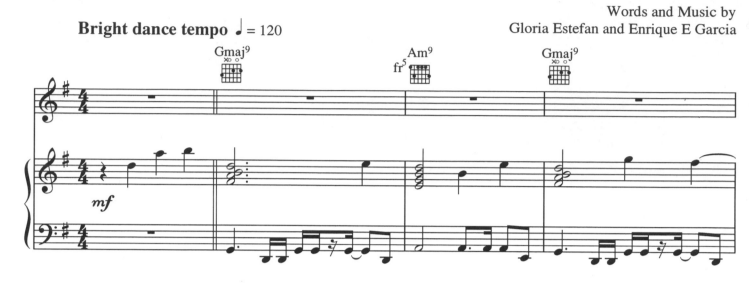

1. They tell me—you're shy, boy,— but I want you just the same.—
2. Come out of— your shell, boy,— you know we go like hand in glove.—
3. *Instrumental Solo ad lib.*

© 1987 & 2000 Foreign Imported Productions & Publishing Inc, USA
EMI Songs Ltd, London WC2H 0EA

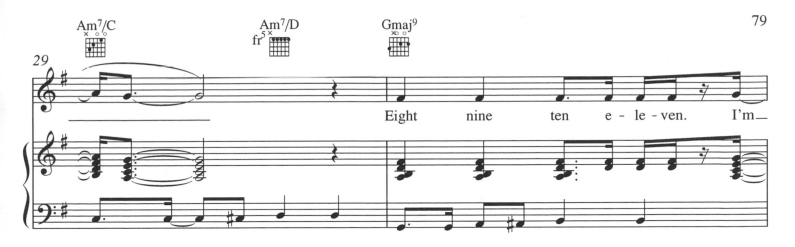

Eight nine ten e - le - ven. I'm

____ just gon - na keep__ on count - ing un - til you are mine.__

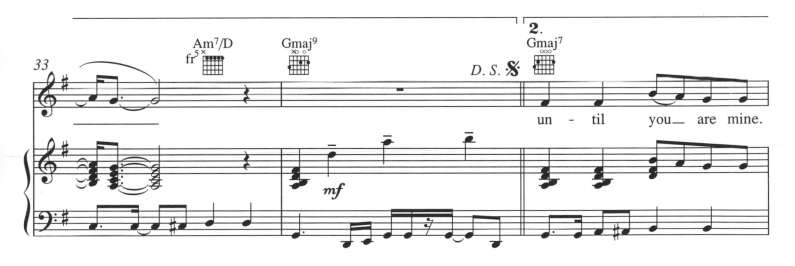

un - til you__ are mine.

un - til you are mine.____

# All The Woman Series

## Woman
### All
### volume one

Contents include: All Woman; Do You Know Where You're Going To?; Ev'ry Time We Say Goodbye;
Fever; I Am What I Am; I Will Always Love You; Miss You Like Crazy; Summertime;
Superwoman; What's Love Got To Do With It and Why Do Fools Fall In Love.
Order Ref: 19076

## Woman
### All
### volume two

Contents include: Don't It Make My Brown Eyes Blue; Giving You The Best That I Got;
Killing Me Softly With His Song; Memory; One Moment In Time; Pearl's A Singer;
That Ole Devil Called Love; Walk On By; The Wind Beneath My Wings and You Don't Have To Say You Love Me.
Order Ref: 2043A

## Woman
### All
### volume three

Contents include: Almaz; Big Spender; Crazy For You; Fame; The First Time Ever I Saw Your Face;
From A Distance; Love Letters; My Baby Just Cares For Me; My Funny Valentine; The Power Of Love;
Promise Me; Saving All My Love For You and Total Eclipse Of The Heart.
Order Ref: 2444A

## Woman
### All
### volume four

Contents include: Anything For You; Evergreen; For Your Eyes Only; I Will Survive; Mad About The Boy;
A Rainy Night in Georgia; Send In The Clowns; Smooth Operator; Sophisticated Lady; Stay With Me Till Dawn;
Sweet Love; Think Twice and Touch Me In The Morning.
Order Ref: 3034A

## Woman
### All
### Blues

Contents include: Body and Soul; Georgia On My Mind; God Bless' The Child;
I Don't Stand A Ghost Of A Chance With You; I Gotta Right To Sing The Blues; I'd Rather Go Blind;
Lover Man (Oh, Where Can You Be?); Mood Indigo; Stormy Weather and You've Changed.
Order Ref: 3690A

## Woman
### All
### Cabaret

Contents include: Almost Like Being In Love; Another Openin', Another Show; Anything Goes;
For Once In My Life; Goldfinger; I Won't Last A Day Without You; If My Friends Could See Me Now;
My Way; New York New York; People and There's No Business Like Show Business.
Order Ref: 3691A

## Woman
### All
### Jazz

Contents include: Bewitched; Crazy He Calls Me; A Foggy Day; Girl From Ipanema; How High The Moon;
I'm In The Mood For Love; It Don't Mean A Thing (If It Ain't Got That Swing); It's Only A Paper Moon;
Misty; On Green Dolphin Street; 'Round Midnight and Straighten Up And Fly Right.
Order Ref: 4778A